DO YOU WANT A PET FERRET?

THAT'S AN ODD PET!

BY LOUIS MALLORY

Enslow PUBLISHING

Please visit our website, www.enslow.com. For a free color catalog of all our high-quality books, call toll free 1-800-398-2504 or fax 1-877-980-4454.

Cataloging-in-Publication Data

Names: Mallory, Louis.
Title: Do you want a pet ferret? / Louis Mallory.
Description: Buffalo, NY : Enslow Publishing, 2025. | Series: That's an odd pet! | Includes glossary and index.
Identifiers: ISBN 9781978540774 (pbk.) | ISBN 9781978540781 (library bound) | ISBN 9781978540798 (ebook)
Subjects: LCSH: Ferrets as pets–Juvenile literature.
Classification: LCC SF459.F47 M35 2025 | DDC 636.976'628–dc23

Published in 2025 by
Enslow Publishing
2544 Clinton Street
Buffalo, NY 14224

Portions of this work were originally authored by Mia Bennett and published as *Ferrets*. All new material in this edition is authored by Louis Mallory.

Designer: Claire Zimmermann
Editor: Natalie Humphrey

Photo credits: Cover (photo) Arnaud NAJARRO/Shutterstock.com; Series Art (title and heading font, texture) Gleb Guralnyk/Shutterstock.com; Series Art (background retro swirl) ChekmanDaria/Shutterstock.com; Series Art (corner dots) Romanova Ekaterina/Shutterstock.com; Series Art (body text boxes, page number background shape) Angie Makes/Shutterstock.com; Series Art (hand-drawn doodles) yugoro/Shutterstock.com; pp. 5, 9 Couperfield/Shutterstock.com; p. 7 Kerry Hargrove/Shutterstock.com; p. 11 AJSTUDIO PHOTOGRAPHY/Shutterstock.com; pp. 13, 15 Irina Vasilevskaia/Shutterstock.com; p. 17 Tom Lester/Shutterstock.com; p. 19 Yasmins world/Shutterstock.com.

Printed in the United States of America

CPSIA compliance information: Batch #CSENS25: For further information contact Enslow Publishing at 1-800-398-2504.

CONTENTS

Words in the glossary appear in **bold** type the first time they are used in the text.

A PET BANDIT

Would you like to add a playful bandit to your family? Then a ferret might be the perfect pet for you! Ferrets have a **reputation** for being mischievous, or playful with a wish to cause trouble. Many ferrets like to steal and hide things from their owners.

JUST THE FACTS!

Always check state and local laws before picking out a pet. In some states, like California and Hawaii, it's illegal to own ferrets!

Ferrets are intelligent animals. They were once used by people to hunt small **rodents** and rabbits. Today, most ferrets kept by people are pets.

WILD FERRETS

Ferrets are cousins of otters and badgers. These animals are all part of the weasel family. **Domesticated** ferrets are meant to be pets, but there are some ferrets still living in the wild.

JUST THE FACTS!

Wild black-footed ferrets are endangered because most of the land where they live and hunt is being used for crops. Endangered means they are in danger of disappearing from the world!

Black-footed ferrets look very similar to pet ferrets, but they're still wild and need to be left alone.

Wild black-footed ferrets live in North America. They mostly hunt at night and eat prairie dogs. Wild ferrets like prairie dogs so much, 90 percent of their food is prairie dogs! When they can't catch prairie dogs, they will eat squirrels, mice, and other small animals.

LONG BODIES

Ferrets aren't big animals. They usually weigh less than 5 pounds (2.3 kg). Their long, thin bodies help them fit into tight spaces. They may have been domesticated for their ability to hunt rodents. They can easily follow rodents into **burrows** under the ground.

Pet ferrets come in many colors. Albino ferrets are white with pink eyes. Many ferrets have a mix of brown and cream-colored fur. The most common ferret color is sable.

JUST THE FACTS!

If you've seen a ferret at a pet store, you've probably seen a sable-colored ferret! These ferrets have tan coats with dark brown or black **guard hairs** and a dark mask around their eyes.

FERRET HOMES

Wild black-footed ferrets live in **abandoned** prairie dog burrows. They also find homes in burrows left behind by other animals.

Just like wild ferrets, your pet ferret needs plenty of places to run and hide. It also needs a comfortable place to sleep. Ferret cages should be large and can have more than one level. These different levels can help you keep your ferret's bed, litter box, and food apart.

Many ferret owners will give their ferret a hammock to sleep in like the one here, but ferrets can also sleep in T-shirts, towels, and blankets!

JUST THE FACTS!

Ferrets are the most comfortable in warm places between about 60° and 80°F (15.5° and 26.7°C).

MEAT EATERS

Ferrets have sharp teeth and only eat meat. This means they are carnivores. Because of that, you need to feed your pet ferret food that's high in **protein**. Many people purchase special high-protein ferret food. Other people feed their ferrets raw or cooked chicken.

Ferrets eat many times throughout the day. Ferrets burn off the food they eat very quickly. Keep food out for your ferret so it can eat whenever it feels hungry.

If you want to give your ferret a treat, you can feed it cooked eggs or raw eggs.

JUST THE FACTS!

Ferrets can eat many kinds of food, but they shouldn't be given fruits, vegetables, dairy, or sugar. Ferrets' stomachs can't **digest** these foods, and they might get sick!

KEEPING YOUR FERRET HEALTHY

Pet ferrets usually live for around five to seven years. Just like cats and dogs, you can give your ferret **vaccinations** to help them stay healthy. You can also give your ferret special **medication** to help prevent **parasites** like fleas and heartworms.

JUST THE FACTS!

If you notice your ferret acting differently than it usually does, like sleeping longer or not eating as much, be sure to talk to an adult.

Taking your ferret to the veterinarian once a year can help keep it healthy.

Regularly taking your pet ferret to the veterinarian can also help it stay healthy. Veterinarians are animal doctors. Ask your veterinarian questions about your ferret so you know how to give it the best care!

A FERRET ADVENTURE!

Ferrets like to explore and have fun! They're playful, curious, and social animals. Ferrets like to play with other ferrets. They'll also play with other small animals like cats. But ferrets should never be left alone with other animals.

JUST THE FACTS!

Ferrets need time to play outside of their cages. Some people will even take their ferret on a walk outside!

Some pet stores sell special ferret **harnesses** to safely take your ferret on a walk.

Ferrets are very smart. You can train them to do simple tasks and use a litter box. Ferrets can also figure out puzzle games. Ferrets love to run through tubes and tunnels. They also love moving toys that make noise.

FERRET PROOFING

Because ferrets need time to explore outside of their cages, make sure your ferret's play area is ferret proof! Expect your ferret to get into places where it doesn't belong.

JUST THE FACTS!

Ferret cages need good locks, otherwise your ferret might escape.

Ferrets should play for two to four hours outside of their cage every day.

Only let your ferret explore in places where it can't get into too much trouble. Try getting down on your ferret's level and seeing what it can see. If you spot a place it can run and hide, try covering it so your ferret can't get inside.

FERRET SAFETY

Because of their high energy and mischief, ferrets can be hard to handle. Ferrets have sharp teeth and can sometimes bite. Ferrets won't usually make you sick. Sometimes, though, ferrets and their poop can carry illness. After handling your ferret, make sure to wash your hands with warm soap and water.

If you take good care of your ferret, it can be a great companion. This fun-loving furry friend may make the perfect addition to your family!

TAKING CARE OF YOUR FERRET!

Make sure your ferret's cage has a good lock and bars that are close together.

Make sure your ferret has places to jump, hide, and climb in their cage.

Feed your ferret high-protein food.

Hold your ferret gently.

Make sure your ferret has fresh water to drink.

Fully clean your ferret's cage once a week.

Make sure to scoop your ferret's litter box daily.

Take your ferret to the veterinarian once a year.

JUST THE FACTS!

Ferrets will steal nearly anything they can fit in their mouths! Check your ferret's cage after it is done exploring to make sure it didn't take anything it shouldn't have.

GLOSSARY

abandon: To leave empty or uncared for.

burrow: A hole in the ground an animal uses to live in or hide in.

digest: To break down food inside the body so that the body can use it.

domesticated: Bred and raised for use by people.

guard hairs: Long, rough hairs that make up the outer layer of an animal's fur.

harness: Straps around an animal that allow a person to control it.

medication: A drug taken to make a sick person or animal well.

parasite: A living thing that lives in, on, or with another living thing, causing harm.

protein: A nutrient in many types of food that the body uses to grow, repair tissues, and stay healthy.

reputation: The views that are held about someone or something.

rodent: A small, furry animal with large front teeth, such as a mouse or rat.

vaccination: To give an animal or person a substance that helps to protect against an illness or disease.

FOR MORE INFORMATION

Books

Koestler-Grack, Rachel A. *Black-Footed Ferrets.* Minneapolis, MN: Bellwether Media, 2023.

Rossiter, Brienna. *My Pet Ferret.* Mendota Heights, MN: Little Blue House, 2023.

Websites

AZ Animals: 10 Incredible Ferret Facts
www.a-z-animals.com/blog/10-incredible-ferret-facts/
Find out more facts about ferrets.

The Nature Conservancy: Black-footed Ferret
www.nature.org/en-us/get-involved/how-to-help/animals-we-protect/black-footed-ferret/
Find out more about wild black-footed ferrets and what people are doing to save them.

Publisher's note to educators and parents: Our editors have carefully reviewed these websites to ensure that they are suitable for students. Many websites change frequently, however, and we cannot guarantee that a site's future contents will continue to meet our high standards of quality and educational value. Be advised that students should be closely supervised whenever they access the internet.

INDEX